PLATFORM PAPERS

QUARTERLY ESSAYS ON THE PERFORMING ARTS FROM CURRENCY HOUSE

No. 49
November 2016

CURRENCY HOUSE

Platform Papers Partners

Platform Papers

Readers' Forum

Readers' responses to our previous essays are posted on our website. Contributions to the conversation (250 to 2000 words) may be emailed to info@currencyhouse. org.au. The Editor welcomes opinion and criticism in the interest of healthy debate but reserves the right to monitor where necessary.

Platform Papers, quarterly essays on the performing arts, is published every February, May, August and November and is available through bookshops, by subscription and online in paper or electronic version. For details see our website at www.currencyhouse.org.au.

Advice to Subscribers

The Platform Paper, *Rethinking the Screen Documentary*, due for publication this month, has been postponed due to illness. We expect to publish it in 2017. Enquiries regarding this title may be made to Currency House at admin@currencyhouse.org.au.

THE LIGHTING DESIGNER: WHAT IS 'GOOD LIGHTING'?

||||||||||||||||||||||||||||||||||||||||||||||||||||||||||||||||||||||||||||||||

NIGEL LEVINGS

ABOUT THE AUTHOR

Nigel Levings is one of Australia's leading theatre lighting designers and in his early career was the first to be fully employed by an Australian theatre company as a lighting designer. In a distinguished career he has lit over 490 original productions including 174 operas and 28 musicals. He has lit opera in St Petersburg, Paris, Washington, London, Cardiff, Berlin, Baden Baden, Innsbruck, Bregenz, New York, Los Angeles, Chicago, Houston, Dallas, Seoul and Toronto as well as all the major opera houses of Australia.

His awards for lighting design include the Helpmann and Green Room Awards, the Los Angeles Ovation Award and the Canadian Dora Mava Moore Award. On Broadway he has won two Outer Circle Critics Awards, a Drama Desk and a Tony Award. He was awarded the Centenary Federation Medal by the Australian Government for his services to opera lighting and, in 2003, was honoured by the SA Great – Arts Award.

Recent work includes: *Die tote Stadt, Of Mice and Men* and the world premiere of *Bliss* for Opera Australia: *Maria de Buenos Aires* for Victorian Opera; *Romeo et Juliette* for Korea National Opera; *The Book of Everything* at the New Victory Theatre, New York; *The King and I* for Opera Australia and Gordon Frost; *Cloudstreet* for State Opera of South Australia, *Disgraced* for Melbourne Theatre Company; *Machu Picchu* for State Theatre Company of South Australia; *Don Carlos* for Opera Australia.

ACKNOWLEDGEMENTS

Parts of this paper were first developed as a keynote address for a conference held by OISTAT on Stage Lighting Design in Hangzhou, China in 2011. Another section was prepared and delivered at the SPARC Conference held as part of the VIVID Festival in 2014. These events sparked my interest in putting on paper my memories of an unexpected life in the dark rooms of the theatres of the world.

For this paper I owe an enormous debt of gratitude to John Senczuk who took my overlong, rambling early draft and made a concise, readable edition. I also want to thank John for his meticulous attention to historical detail and for correcting a long-standing misapprehension about the venue for the production of *Camelot*. Also to Katharine Brisbane for first approaching me and then encouraging and supporting me as this paper took shape.

Preface

When you watch a great ballet dancer there is an overwhelming sense of effortlessness. You simply cannot see them putting in an effort. Every step looks absolutely inevitable. This is a quality to which I aspire in my lighting. Inevitable and effortless …

We say, 'Let's go to the theatre and see a show.' Some nights when I see a show I come away with steam coming out of my ears, incensed by what I have seen on stage—or, to be precise, incensed by what I have not seen. As a lighting designer the thing I find impossible to forgive is not seeing the actors. I worked many times with the notoriously difficult director Ian Judge whose reputation struck fear into the hearts of actors and stage crew alike. I continued to work with him over many years because I liked his productions and he always made me laugh. He is a very witty man whose razor sharp tongue confirmed his reputation with those at the receiving end of his savage critiques. But every time I sit at the production desk lighting a show the memory of his voice rings in my ears: 'Can't see 'em.' He was usually right, of course, and his whip-crack comments forced me to focus on my fundamental function in the production. Like a lot of great directors, diplomacy was never a skill he aspired to master and consequently he rarely works these days.

When I see a production where the lighting designer has obviously had more concern for the character of the stage picture than the visibility of the performer I become deeply irritated and sometimes find myself doing stupid things like writing ill-tempered letters to the artistic director (I never had another offer from that company). So I set myself the challenge to write down what I believe theatre lighting should aspire to attain. Like a philosopher, I set off in search of the answer to the question: 'What is good lighting?' Where does quality exist in lighting for the stage? Where do lighting designers come from? My paper poses the question from various points of view—the audience, the author, the critic, the designers, the director and finally from my own point of view. Ultimately it is of course a subjective answer but it's clear that there are certain objective elements: visibility being one; and integration with the rest of the design another.

1. This Lighting Designer

I grew up in Melbourne and in primary school our Year 6 teacher, Mr Edgar Seppings, gave me my first brush with the theatre. I was too young at the time for much recall but I do remember the magic of that lit space and the surrounding darkness. A warm sunny glade into which I emerged from the dark burrows of the backstage world, nose twitching, ears swiveling.

My parents took me to the theatre in the early 1960s. I saw *Camelot*[1] at Her Majesty's Theatre and particularly vivid in my memory is a scene in the cave of Morgan Le Fey. The curtain rose and silhouetted against a vivid red sky was a rope net with dancers clinging to it. Black shapes against the red sky—an image of spiders on a web or perhaps the trussed bodies of victims.[2] Looking up from my seat in the stalls I was entranced by two thick, almost tangible, beams of blue light coming from behind me. I turned to look and fell in love with those two follow-spot beams etched in the darkness and pouring silently down onto the stage below.

In later years at high school I became involved with the local amateur drama group. I did a bit of acting, young Patrick in *Auntie Mame* was my main claim to fame, and eventually a bit of lighting. A small resistance dimmer board on a perch position behind the proscenium provided a fascinating view of the stage. Looking down on that broadly lit space, seeing in one view the transition from the darkness and secrecy of the backstage world to the evocation of a world encased in our painted flats and found furniture, was a thrilling experience. And when Colin, the lighting operator, got me to operate one of the slider dimmers I was hooked. How miraculous: you pushed this lever up here and over there the light swelled and the stage came to life.

At University I studied law and helped pay my way with part-time work in the theatre. This was in the heady days of the late 1960s when campus revolution was in the air and when the seeds of Australia's new wave of theatre were being planted. In Melbourne it was the time of La Mama and the Pram Factory and all my friends were part of this world. Although I found myself working in the mainstream theatre I always understood and empathized with the aspirations of 'poor' theatre. Initially I worked just at Monash University's Alexander Theatre but later at various commercial theatres around Melbourne. Mostly I worked at the Princess Theatre as part of the lighting crew. There was no such thing as a lighting designer in those days. The lighting was 'done' by someone with aptitude, authority—and another job. It was the wonderful Bill Akers, stage manager and lighting designer at the Australian Ballet, whose impeccable mastery of colour I have always sought to emulate. The Australian Opera's visits to the Princess were invariably lit by Tony Everingham. Otherwise it was usually a stage manager or production manager but sometimes the production electrician translated and relayed the desires of the director and set designer. I soon discovered that I had quite an aptitude for focusing lights and was a pretty good lighting operator. The Princess in those days had a lighting desk called the CD, which stood not for compact disk but 'clutch dimmer'. It was a mighty beast not unlike an organ console with foot switches and magnetic latches and an accelerator pedal to control the speed of the lighting transitions. Theatre eventually lured me away from my law studies, which had in the meantime become arts/law. Studying plays in the English literature course made me think how out of water these texts seemed when they were simply read and not performed on the stage. But it was always the literature of theatre that drew me in. As a shy, tongue-tied young man I found in theatre a world where people could communicate: a world where the complex and unsaid thoughts running through my mind found articulate expression in the words of others.

After what seemed a relatively short time as one of the lighting assistants to the head electrician at the Princess Theatre, I was offered the position of head of lighting for the Melbourne Theatre Company at Russell Street Theatre. I joined the company at the beginning of 1971 and my first production there was *The Government Inspector* [3] directed by George Ogilvie and featuring Robin Ramsay in the title role. Robin was at that stage a big TV star through his appearances on the popular ABC soap opera *Bellbird*. I was in Russell Street for three years operating the control system, maintaining the equipment and rigging the lights. But most importantly for me I had the opportunity to begin designing the lighting. This was not the process we understand today. I would put together a rudimentary pencilled drawing of a lighting plan which I hoped would meet the requirements of the director. I would rig and focus this largely on my own and then in technical sessions sit at the lighting desk responding to the director's requests. As I got better I would offer more and more visual suggestions. But at that stage there were still no lighting design credits; my title was 'electrician'.

After three years at the MTC I needed to find out more about the craft of lighting design. There were no courses to study in Australia but there were the beginnings of degree courses at some American universities. So I planned a study tour and applied for an Australia Council travel grant.

The study tour started in 1974 with a stint with Theatre Projects [TP] in London. At the time Richard Pilbrow had established a sort of atelier of lighting designers that worked alongside his lighting equipment hire business. My steepest learning curve at TP was drafting. It is something I had never learnt. My MTC plans had been little crosses and arrows on a printed copy of the set plan. At TP I was expected to draft in ink on drafting paper on a proper drawing board and using the proprietary lighting stencils developed at TP. I rapidly learnt the use of the razor blade to scratch out my smudges and errors. But I was fortunate to work with a number of designers on various projects around London, drafting in the office or taking notes in the theatre; keeping them company in the pubs or simply watching Richard himself, or his colleagues Bob Ornbo, Nick Chelton, Howard Eldridge and John B. Read. Later I went to the Nottingham Playhouse in the time when Richard Eyre was director, and worked with the resident lighting designer, Geoffrey Mercereau. A popular regional theatre of modern design, it seemed the model most relevant to the changes going on in Australian theatre at that time.

The next part of my trip took me to New York where I did what I think you might call an internship with Jules Fisher, the great lighting designer. I worked on a number of projects with Jules including the 1975 production of *Chicago*[4] which I observed at its Philadelphia try-out. So ignorant was I, I did not realise that the director sitting next to Jules was Bob Fosse or that the two gals up on stage were Gwen Vernon and Chita Rivera. Jules Fisher has won more Tony awards than any other lighting designer. Working with him was a remarkable lesson in professionalism and a far cry from the pub-centred world of London lighting designers where 'the Behan myth'[5] of the drunken genius still held sway. One lesson that I learned from Jules was to think about the light and not the lighting instrument. Work out what effect you wanted on stage and then calculate the type of instrument you needed. This was the reverse of the 'seat of the pants' approach to choosing instruments that I had been used to employing. After that there were further visits to Stratford Ontario and Tyrone Guthrie's famous stage; and at the end of my trip an immersion in the world of rock-and-roll lighting in San Francisco.

On my return to Australia I was, after an anxious period of under-employment, offered a position with George Ogilvie at the South Australian Theatre Company.[6] I joined the company in mid-1975 and became the first resident lighting designer in Australia. There had been other designers before me who had 'done' the lighting for a company but I was the first full-time, salaried employee at any theatre company in Australia employed solely to design the lighting for all the productions in the season. There I stayed, honing my craft for nearly a decade—working under the artistic directorships of Colin George, Kevin Palmer, and with Jim Sharman's infamous Lighthouse Company before taking the plunge into the precarious world of the freelance lighting designer. In 1984 I joined a small cohort of intrepid young practitioners who—although we didn't realise it at the time—were blazing a trail in the Australian theatre. Among them I had always felt an affinity with Roger Barratt.

I remember us sharing our aspirations when Roger was working as Les Bowden's assistant at the Australian Opera and I was the lighting operator at the Princess. Lighting—we didn't add the suffix 'design' in those days—was what we both wanted to do. Bill Akers, the technical director at the Australian Ballet, was the older master whose elegant style we so admired. Previously he was credited as stage manager and lighting designer I was amazed at his lighting for the ballet *Sun Music*.[7] I still remember the opening sequence: a pile of bodies on the stage with slowly moving dots of light revolving over them. Bill had concealed a mirror ball between two borders and by lighting across it from the fly floors had produced these mysterious dots.

The biggest difficulty about going freelance was losing the security of a regular job, of losing an office in which to work and all those everyday necessities, phones and drafting boards and paper and ink etc. paid for by someone else. My first freelance opera was a production of *La Sonnambula*[8] for the Italian Arts Festival in 1978, directed by Franco Cavarra. Franco had a successful career in theatre and opera and was influential in the Melbourne Italian community before entering the priesthood in later life. My work was often with directors I had worked with in Adelaide but not in all cases. I first worked with Neil Armfield on *Volpone*[9] for the Nimrod Theatre Company in Sydney in 1980 and that later became an important working partnership.

Although I was conscious of the politics at the time, I did not think much about the Australian Opera's policy towards creative imports. Some of my earliest work with them was as the Australian component of an otherwise international team. I first worked with the great Göran Järvefelt and his designer Carl Friedrich Oberle when the Australian Opera[10] asked me to light their production of *The Magic Flute*.[11] But the bulk of my theatrical work from this time was with Nimrod at their Belvoir Street Theatre, and with Sydney Theatre Company. I had been doing some opera with State Opera in SA since 1982 (including *Falstaff*[12] directed by Colin George) but my first production for the Australian Opera was *Fidelio*[13] in 1984 in a re-studied production by Elke Neidhardt performed in the old Allan Lees set.

Internationally my career started in 1994 with a production of *A Christmas Carol*[14] for the Royal Shakespeare Company at the Barbican. I had been invited to light the production after working with Ian Judge on his production of *West Side Story*[15] at the Princess. His reputation has previously been referred to as fearsome but we hit it off fabulously and continued working together for many years in many parts of the world.

My process

As soon as a potential project comes up in discussion, I begin my process. I start to research all I can about the work, the venue, the company and my colleagues on the creative team and the cast. If it is an opera with an available recording I will start to listen to it in detail. If the piece is based on another form of literature I will read the source material. Usually I start this research process well before I begin to discuss the directorial approach— the concept—to the work. I need to come to my own understanding of the script and of the team with whom I will be working. I make notes about the work and the structure of the piece, paying particular attention to any mention of light conditions. I believe very strongly in the primacy of the text. Sometimes when I see productions that so deliberately play at odds with what is written I feel deeply angry. If you do not agree with Chekhov's conclusions or characters then write your own bloody play, don't trade on somebody else's words or reputation.

How soon the design process starts, however, varies from production to production. Opera companies used to contract their creatives more than two years in advance but these days the advance time frame is severely reduced. Theatre companies, too, are inclined to leave the lighting contract until the last minute, which means that work offers come in a rush before next season's brochure goes to the printer. Perhaps this is a cash flow management issue for theatre companies: they will be required to pay a percentage of the lighting designer's fee upfront to secure their services, and importantly their availability, for rehearsals and the technical production period.

I care deeply about how the stage is lit and work hard to ensure that all elements of the production are speaking the same language. I saw two productions by the Scottish opera director Sir David McVicar recently and they encapsulate everything I hate about this type of theatre. Firstly I could not see the singers, either in the *Don Giovanni* or the *Cosi Fan Tutte*.[16] He seemed not to give a stuff about singers wandering around trying to act in the dark. Secondly, in the *Cosi* for example, he chose to ignore everything Mozart had put into the lovers' final reconciliation music in order to make some point about an ongoing bitter struggle in the relationships. It's not that I intrinsically object to *regietheater*.[17] Who could after seeing the brilliant Chéreau *Ring*?[18] I just object when directors don't listen to the text. In some hands these strong directorial statements can work wonderfully to elucidate the text. I did an *Orfeo*[19] with Barrie Kosky many years ago and I recall one scene in which he had the chorus tapping pencils while they all tried to emulate Orfeo creating his music. There was a sort of jazz syncopation in the pencil tapping that made it immediately clear that this music of Monteverdi was where jazz came from—the birth of the cool many centuries before it hit New York.

The actual process of 'designing' is relatively simple: you read a script and come to understand the time and place in which the text is set; you analyse the geometry of available lighting positions set by the theatre architecture and by the strictures imposed by the set; you discuss with your colleagues the overall creative approach to the work. In most instances you will then have to prepare a lighting drawing on this basis, particularly if it is a commercial musical. If you are careful you will leave enough wiggle room in the drawing of this rig to take account of developments in the rehearsal room. But in most cases during the rehearsal process you will be looking to see how you can create the lighting imagery from the equipment allocation represented in your lighting drawing.

Working relationships with directors are as varied as any other human relationship. The briefings can be succinct over a coffee or drawn out over weeks. Ultimately it is hard to talk about lighting, the broad approach is usually clear from the set design presentation but the myriad details of transitions and colour tones and visibility gradients can really only be seen when the production is on stage. Sometimes there will be endless discussions and trials of certain effects. The opera *Die tote Stadt*[20] requires that a portrait of a character's dead wife comes to life. The director Bruce Beresford and I experimented a lot with a holographic projection technology called *Musion* which is a contemporary variation of the old theatre trick called 'Pepper's Ghost'.[21] In the end we abandoned this option as it only worked for a limited audience angle of view. It was not going to work for the cheap seats.

Directors have many answers to the question of what is good lighting. One such answer might be 'lighting that I do not have to do myself'. It is my thesis that the role of the lighting designer developed when the range of equipment and complexity of control got beyond the conditions in which the task could be accomplished by the director and the set designer shouting at the theatre electrician. Today lighting systems allow for an extraordinary level of control over the components of the lighting rig; but such flexibility requires detailed planning and a considerable specialist aptitude for the task. Some directors like to micro-manage all aspects of a performance from the angle of the actor's hand to the intensity of any one of several hundred lighting instruments. Personally I try to avoid working with these directors. It is clear that they do not really need me and would be happier with an electrician to shout at. My general advice to such directors is that if you get a dog, you do not need to bark yourself.

Directors rehearse performances in spaces where every area of the marked-out space has equal value in terms of its illumination. Into this space they try to create a traffic of the stage that brings to light the internal relationships of the characters and the meaning of the text. By the end of the rehearsal process a pattern of movement around the stage is relatively fixed. In opposition to this is the fact that human beings are phototropic animals. In other words our everyday movements and the positions we adopt in the world are dependent on the lighting conditions in which we find ourselves. In most instances we subconsciously avoid glare, we read where the light is best, we listen intently in the dark. In winter we seek the warmth of the sun, in summer the shade of the trees. As an exercise in power we like to have our backs to the window so others cannot see our face but we can see theirs; at our dinner tables we like a warm interior glow and are comforted by the cosiness induced by the darkness surrounding us. No matter how old and wise we get there is always a residual fear of the absolute dark and all the associations of the unseen that it brings to mind. None of the vast range of human phototropic responses to light are dealt with in the rehearsal space. So it is part of the lighting designer's task to reverse engineer an emotional architecture of light in the space when no such motivation has been there as part of the rehearsal process.

Many times I have seen directors unhappy with one particular aspect of their work—and in even more cases with particular aspects of an actor's performance. At these times a director's view of 'good lighting' might be that which puts the weaker aspects of the production in the dark. Lighting designers are sometimes called 'The Princes of Darkness'. Not guilty! In my career it has always been the director who has asked for less light or more darkness. Opera directors are particularly prone to this as they are usually not responsible for the casting and find it easy to blame the performers. To elicit the best work from other members of the creative team, the director needs to encourage their active contribution. It is only when directors can persuade their team that the text in hand is important, and the project valid, that we are in with a chance to create something worthwhile. To enthuse the creative team with their vision of the work enables the director to bring out the best responses from their team. As far as the lighting is concerned this should be something much better than they have ever personally imagined. The set design is sketched and modelled and discussed through many drafts until the ideas and the approach are clear. The costume designs also go through many drafts before they are carefully drawn and presented; but light cannot be modelled: it is extremely difficult to even discuss the lighting in other than broad terms. For the director, in this case, good lighting is that which takes the ideas and spirit of the work developed in the rehearsal studio, expands and surprises with its interpretation. An elegant and appropriate flow of light from one cue to the next will count highly as good lighting with a director. Most of them spend so much rehearsal time concentrating on the rhythm of the work that an ability to move at the appropriate pace will be highly valued. So we arrive at the understanding that the integration of the lighting into the overall production is fundamental to any mark of quality in the design. How well have the creative team played together? How good is the fit?

I prepare a lighting plan indicating the placement of my chosen lighting equipment in the space. I used to write what I called a 'shot list', a list of all those things I needed the lighting design to achieve. My drafting process would then be to draw circles in pencil over a printed copy of the set design plan. These circles represented areas of lighting control. I would give them a letter designation and then go about adding lights to cover the areas, crossing them off my shot list as they went on to the drawing. The rough draft would have a small cross to represent the light position, an arrow indicating the direction it was pointing, a letter to designate the area it was to light and a colour filter number. After the draft process I would place drafting paper over the plan and proceed with stencils and ink to draw the final plan.

From my plan the lighting crew rig and interconnect all this equipment. Then I come to the stage and direct the focus of each individual lighting instrument according to my 'design' intentions. Once all these elements are there on stage I finally have the palette of possibilities in place and can begin creating the lighting cues from various combinations of these lights at various intensities. I then rehearse and adjust the flow of the lighting images. I polish and re-jig and amend and re-consider and sometimes start again, until I finish—or more often run out of time. I then collect my cheque and move on to the next job.

2. The Craft of Lighting Design

It takes an unusual combination of skills and interests to be a lighting designer. We have one foot in the world of the sciences; and the urban myths of our society tell us that people interested in technical things don't read books, listen to classical music or enjoy art of any sort. Yet we are also artists and deeply interested in all forms of human artistic creativity. I think this straddling of two worlds, left brain and right brain, technology and art—develops or perhaps attracts those with some very interesting sets of skills. Those who are drawn to it will be deeply in love with the silent magic of light. They will see in the theatre an art form where they can be part of a community of people striving to present before an audience some expression of our common humanity a mutual reassurance that we are not alone.

Light is the tool with which we create our designs and the lighting designer must fully understand the workings of this tool before they can begin to realise the lighting imagery they wish to create on the stage. Lighting designers stand at the gateway between the external world of the stage action and the internal worlds of our audience. We control the flow of knowledge available to the audience during the passage of the play, we stand between what the actor is trying to convey with their face and body and what the audience perceive. The audience's perception of the action on stage occurs not as an image projected on their retina but as an image formed in their brains; and hence this image is subject to the multiplicity of associations and life experience that our audience has accumulated. Ultimately it is these associations in our audience that we are attempting to trigger. The storm that King Lear undergoes on that blasted heath becomes so much more resonant for the audience when, instead of a physical manifestation, the lighting designer touches elements that trigger the storm of their imagination.

We interpret the world through a combination of what we detect visually through the impact of reflected light on our retina and what we have learned about the world. The simplest illustration of this is contained in our mental image of night. Movie makers, in the days when cameras needed massive amounts of light to expose their film, would shoot 'day for night', a blue tint applied to images shot in daylight and underexposed, suggesting moonlight. Blue light on a stage might suggest night to our audience's imagination, which will fill in the gaps and load the image with their own personal associations. This mental association is partly to do with the wavelengths of light to which we are most sensitive—the cooler end of the blue-green part of the spectrum. But 'day for night' is just a suggestion triggering our mental understanding of night; the reality is that a dark night has no colour.

The colour receptors in our retina are known as cone receptors and although they can detect a high level of detail and colour they require a certain level of light to function. Our visual system also contains rod type receptors which are highly sensitive to low levels of light but have no colour discrimination. Below a certain level of illumination our vision is what is termed *scotopic*, only the rod receptors are sending signals to the brain. We see but have no sense of colour, only varying levels of luminance. Scotopic vision is very sensitive to movement and, since our rod receptors are more strongly clustered at the edges of our retina, they are extremely sensitive in our peripheral vision. I think of this as the sabre-toothed tiger response—a high level of sensitivity in our peripheral vision at low light levels is a strong survival strategy. Unfortunately it also makes it very hard for a stage crew to make an undetected scene change in a blackout.

Seeing the actor

The physics of light and the biology of vision are intrinsic to the simple illumination of the performance. Arrange the passage of the light from the source to the subject and thence to the viewer. The process of ordering this passage of photons is integral to lighting design.

Lighting designers have come to accept that most audiences have only a vague idea of what their work entails. People are used to making decisions about the clothes they wear, the type of car they drive, the disposition of the furniture in their homes, the gardens they create, the very house in which they live. These are all design decisions and it is relatively easy to transfer this understanding to the processes involved in set or costume design. Light is something that most people take for granted in their daily lives. You turn the switch on the wall and proceed about your business. Audiences rarely consider this, but the design of light on the stage has run through many drafts and been amended over many rehearsals. Most of the time the way that space looks is just accepted, and the new 'look' of the space is credited solely to the set designer. Unless the lighting makes itself obvious it will be largely taken for granted.

Think of painting as an analogy. When we view a painting most of us will assume that the artist has rendered what they see and done so in a particular style. But when we stop to think we begin to understand that everything in the picture plane has been carefully interpreted. Degas did not just paint a snapshot of dancers rehearsing and imitate the prevailing lighting; he composed their limbs in forms and patterns to lead the eye across the canvas. He conveyed in paint not the photographic reality of the lighting but the emotional feel of it. When it is good, stage lighting can be like this.

In the cinema the camera provides a single viewpoint for the audience. Nothing is seen that the director does not wish to be seen; everything is seen in the chosen scale; every image is exposed to the value agreed by the director and the director of photography (DOP) and every action of the actor is exposed to the camera or audience at precisely the angle the director chooses, and at precisely the angle to the incident light that the director and DOP choose. The ability to place a light wherever needed, ignoring what the light does after it has illuminated the object in question; controlling the angle of incidence across the actor's face for a single horizontal and vertical perspective; these are privileges the stage designer can only envy.

How the audience sees an actor is a product of the angle at which the light illuminates the face. The closer the angle of incident light approaches the angle of audience view, the 'flatter' the appearance of the actor becomes. In order to perceive three-dimensional structure we need the light to pass at an angle across the object. Gradations of light intensity, shadows and highlights, reveal the shape of the face or the body. This is how two-dimensional paintings can portray three-dimensional figures. If you can convincingly depict in two dimensions the gradations of light intensity on a three-dimensional figure you have the illusion of a three-dimensional object.

Our understanding of what an actor says is affected by our understanding of the intention they portray with their face and body. Conveying this intention to the audience involves perception of the three-dimensional mobile form of the actor. So the lighting designer's job is to set up this actor/audience communication using a variety of lighting angles situated somewhere along the scale of 'flat' to 'sharp'.

Unfortunately this ideal view of the actor on the stage only works for a single audience member. In most cases it will be that person who happens to be sitting in the seat where the lighting designer sat during the production period. In most theatres there is a wide range of both horizontal and vertical viewpoints available for the audience. Closer more central seats will usually attract a higher ticket price and in one sense these audience members are privileged over the less well-off in that their image of the stage is brighter, more detailed and with clearer and louder diction from the actors. When I lit *La Bohème*[22] on Broadway, sound re-enforcement was used for the singers with the explicit instruction to the sound design team that it was not to sound amplified. The aim was simply to give the audience at the back of the gallery the same acoustic experience as those sitting in the central stalls. This is not an option available to the lighting designer.

Here we come to the first of the compromises the lighting designer faces, or we can settle for only one seat in the house seeing the full intent of the lighting design. Compromise might involve softening some sharp modelling; it might concede to an uncomfortably bright image for the front rows in order to achieve acceptable visibility in the back rows, or it might have to remove certain lighting angles from the range of options because of glare in the side seats. The degree of compromise is weighted according to the style of your production. In my experience: 'high art' productions are allowed to indulge some obscurity, but a commercial comedy must be nice and bright. I was once pleased to observe, while lighting *The King and I*[23] with Hayley Mills as Anna, that when she was on stage I was able to read my notes in the back row of the gallery.

So for the audience the question of what is good lighting is a judgment based on the kind of work you have chosen, the position of the seat you have purchased and what it is you are hoping to see in this performance. A star actor? An immersion in the imaginative creation of some auteur director? A well-told tale? An evening of light entertainment? The fundamental bottom line is still hedged under the illumination of the performance but we edge closer to a basis for a judgment when we consider that the varying degrees of quality are contained in the analysis of how well the lighting is integrated into the performance.

The writer and composer

Playwrights will from time to time get to see how designers interpret their work. In this case they have the chance to exercise their judgment, and ask themselves, is the lighting for their play 'good'? My friend and colleague the stage designer Stephen Curtis, the author of a recent Platform Paper, suggested that stage directions in italics should be ignored unless written by Patrick White;[24] but I disagree. It's true that the author may not be the best judge of how to stage the work they have written but the stage directions are a collection of valuable clues to the meaning of the work. I am particularly interested in the structure that authors build in their plays. The rhythm of scenes is important and sometimes it is not right to ride roughshod over these breaks in an attempt to 'play through' the text.

Lighting designers by habit of professional focus will be reading a text for clues about time and place. One of the fundamental rules for good lighting might be: never make a liar of the actor. If in the course of the dialogue a character refers to the moonlight then it is the lighting designer's responsibility to make sure the audience recognise the reference. In many texts the time of day is of critical importance to the plot. The plays of Shakespeare were written at a time when performances occurred during daylight hours; illumination of the stage made little contribution to the audience's experience. Instead the text carried the whole weight of identifying time and place and the stage picture was elaborated in the audience's imagination. 'Think, when we talk of horses, that you see them printing their proud hoofs i'th' receiving earth.' This very clear indication, from the Prologue in *Henry V,* of the audience's role in the creation of the play, is central to my thesis on triggering the imaginative participation of the theatre audience.

In the first Act of the opera *La Bohème* the scene is set in a Parisian rooftop garret, the home of a group of struggling artists. It is night time on Christmas Eve, Northern Hemisphere. We know from the text that the space is candle-lit, that it has been very cold and that halfway through the scene the bohemians will light a stove with an unexpected gift of firewood. We know also that at least by the end of this scene some beautiful winter moonlight will transfigure the soprano Mimi and send our hero Rodolfo tumbling head over heels in love with her. When they meet he is writing by candlelight in the warmth and perhaps light from the stove, his fellow lodgers having left him alone while they go to the local bar. Mimi, a neighbour, enters with her candle; it has gone out and she does not have a light in her apartment. She is pale from the exertions of her climb and perhaps the incipient consumption that will kill her at the end of the opera, and this causes her to faint. She revives, they talk briefly by the warm fire, he lights her candle and she starts to exit but discovers she has dropped the key to her apartment. As she is standing in the doorway her candle is blown out by the wind. A moment later Rodolfo's candle also goes out—or perhaps he has seized the opportunity and extinguished his own candle. So now the room is quite dark—the Italian word in the text is *buio'*—gloom or blackness. In this gloom they search for her lost key. At one particular point in the music Rodolfo finds the key, exclaims and then quickly hides it in his pocket. A clear expression of his interest in this pale, shy young woman. In their continued searches in the darkness their hands touch and with this touch Rodolfo first comments on her tiny cold hand. Thus begins the first of the two great love arias of the opera.

So here is the lighting dilemma. In a large theatre, with many people viewing the stage from well over thirty metres, how do we convey the sense of a very dark room and yet still reveal to our audience this small but critical gesture of someone finding and then concealing a key? Of this first delicate, accidental—or perhaps deliberate—touch of their hands in the darkness? We must also remember that this is the sort of darkness that liberates feelings, hides blushes and encourages intimacy. It is a snug corner in a bleak and lonely winter; warm, intimate and soon to be bathed in glorious moonlight. A transfiguring moonlight for Mimi that we will come to understand in time foretells her proximity to death. They are doomed from the start. These are the sorts of meanings we must strive to convey with the lighting. Get this right and maybe the composer and librettist would have agreed that we had made 'good lighting'.

Contemporary writing for the theatre does not seem to require such loading of the text with this precisely detailed track of lighting imagery; but care still needs to be taken that the stage lighting echoes the times and places in which the author places the action. Lighting that is evocative of this 'track' will probably be counted as good by the author. Lighting that respects the author's written structure will also get a tick in the good lighting box. Given that the author has the text rattling around inside their head, the issue of actor visibility and consequent audibility may not rank as highly in the good lighting scale of attributes. But evocation of text and unity of structure with the text certainly fall within the criteria of good lighting. Lighting that integrates itself into the production and stitches the elements together into a seamless whole.

The set designer

If the set looks fantastic then the lighting is good. Simple answer to an uncomplicated question? Set designers have the enormous advantage of being able to model the space that they are creating but in most cases they are viewing it under uniform lighting. At one stage in my work with the Australian Opera a regular model lighting session was established during which the set designer and I would explore the possible lighting approaches to the space and photograph the results as reference sources. The limit of this approach was that it could only express broad lighting gestures and was done long before the real work of the director in the rehearsal studio had begun. We were trying to illustrate a possible approach to the lighting without any reference points other than how interesting the set looked. Not how it clarified the text or illuminated the performance or chimed with how the director explored the themes in the rehearsal room.

There are three sorts of surfaces with which the lighting interacts in its passage from source to subject to viewer: the actors' skin, their clothing and the surfaces surrounding the actors' space. In terms of the latter, of paramount importance to me is the quality of the finish of those surfaces. Real surfaces in our world usually have a texture or a 'bite' that affects the light. Diffusely reflective surfaces are often dull when seen over larger distances. Flat painted scenery looks like what it is. Without a certain level of glaze to a painted surface the way the light interacts simply does not ring true. A surface that mixes diffuse and specular reflection allows us to read the colour of the surface tempered with the colour of the incident light that we see because of that specular component. The extreme example of specular reflection is the mirror, the darkest object you can ever place on the stage.

The physical structure of the theatre places limitations on where lights may be rigged. These limitations restrict the range of incident angles available to the lighting designer. The structure of the set further restricts the choices of lighting angles. The one final restriction is a surface finish that forces the lighting designer to light the actors separately from the space in which they are performing. Projection surfaces are one example of this. Light travelling in straight lines will invariably hit the surrounding surfaces after it has accomplished its task of illuminating the performer. If this is rendered out of the question by the nature of the surrounding surfaces then the lighting is severely compromised. Available incident angles can be restricted by the geometry of the theatre, the nature of the scenery, the viewing angles of the audience and now by what happens to the light after it has accomplished its actor-illumination tasks. If the surrounding surface ends up brighter than the actor's face it makes it harder for the audience to 'see' the actor.

Human vision does not work by evenly taking in at a glance the whole scene. Many experiments in which the focus point of the eyes has been tracked show an interesting and very selective view of a scene. In our retina there is an area called the fovea where there is an especially dense collection of cone receptors. It is here that our vision is most precise. If you close one eye, raise your thumb and hold that arm out at full stretch, then your thumbnail roughly represents the area of most visual acuity. Our brain requires details about what we are seeing in order to assemble the complete picture. It does that by selectively moving the focus of this densely packed region of the retina across the surface at which we are looking. The process occurs many times a second and it combines periods of rapid movement called saccades with periods of fixed gaze, called as you might expect, fixation. A series of experiments was carried out in 1965 by the Russian psychologist Alfred Lukyanovich Yarbus in which the subjects were asked to look at a painting by Ilya Repin entitled 'An Unexpected Visitor'.[25] The patterns of their eye movements were detected and later laid over a copy of the painting. The eye jumps from face to face, dwelling longer on the more prominent; but also briefly checking the faces in paintings on the wall and other bright areas. Subjects were then questioned about the people in the paintings and new, very different traces were recorded. Other experiments that look at patterns of saccades and fixation on the human face show similarly strong fixation points on the eyes. Why are we not surprised by that news?

A major part of what lighting is trying to do on stage is to guide this trail of saccades and fixation in accordance with the priorities of the storytelling, as determined by the director and the actors during the rehearsal process. Scanning and sampling is another way to describe the process. This is what painting does: it guides the traverse of the eye across the painted surface by means of the assembled areas of brightness and shapes. The lesson from the Yarbus experiments is that the eye first seeks out the areas in the field of view that most resemble a human face. Face-recognition software on photo applications tries to do the same thing. The prominence of the face in the geometry of the space will decide where the cursory glance will first pause to examine; but if there are questions the brain is seeking to answer then the order of scanning will be different. Brightness of the face will also determine the scanning sequence. Very little fixation occurs on the surrounding surfaces. In this experiment with the Repin painting, only when the subjects were asked to estimate the financial circumstance of the family, or to memorise the family's clothes, was there more fixation on clothing than faces. In all cases the only brief fixations on surrounding surfaces were, like our sometimes aberrant face recognition software, on areas of the 'scenery' that might just have been a face. You will find the same thing with the 'Jesus in the toast' effect: when the brain misinterprets patterns of light and dark as a human face. The point about this is not to denigrate the contribution of the set design to understanding and interpreting the text but simply to explain why the human face is paramount in visual processing.

This is not to imply that the only source of important information we take in is through the fovea; it is in our broader visual receptors that we pick up the clues about the space. An interesting exercise is to look at a good reproduction of the *Mona Lisa*.[26] The enigma of that smile that is not there. Try looking just at the hands. You should find the smile hovering in your peripheral vision. Switch back to the mouth and the smile disappears. The explanation is to do with the higher degree of visual acuity in the foveal area than in the rest of the visual field. The slightly less detailed vision away from the fovea allows the blurred smile to appear. The set does the same thing, hovering in the background of the actor and supplying rich depth of meaning to the text; teasing the brain with suggestions of the world inhabited by the text, and opening out the range of associations.

When considering the question of how to light a set, I first ask what opportunities the set design provides for lighting the actors. Some designs will place severe restraints on the lighting angles available. In this case the best plan of attack is to use those restraints as the key to the style of lighting. Ceilings on a set, for example, are a vertical restriction to the audience's view of the space. Other designs may also have a very strong architectural sense to their work and almost define the very manner in which the space should be lit. But set designers, like directors, are always open to the surprises their stage shapes may reveal when lit in a particular way. The optimum situation for the lighting designer is to integrate the concepts developed in the early director/designer discussion with the much later rehearsal-room-derived approach that comes about through the director/actor developments. The advantage of the lighting design having a last-addition status enables the lighting designer to blend the creative contributions of director and set designer into a coherent whole. When it's good that is.

Colour and the 'frocks'

Lighting and costume designers have much in common in their approach to their work. The lighting designer's overriding concern is with the visibility of the actor's face and with the accurate rendering of skin tones. Costume designers are also concerned with the look of the actor and the balance between skin and costume. So in most instances if the face looks right then the clothes they are wearing will also look right.

Hats are an area where costume designers and lighting designers particularly struggle. Hats are mostly used for status or to keep the sun off your face—an essential marker in many stage environments. But lighting designers want to see the performer's eyes. When the question of hats is raised in the costume design presentation, the fabulous Elaine Stritch comes to mind with that line from the song 'The Ladies Who Lunch' in Sondheim's *Company*[27]: 'Does anyone still wear a hat?'

Costume designers go to great lengths to choose the right fabric. A material with a particular range of colours that precisely matches the designer's understanding of the character can take a very long time to source and when found at the right price can be a triumph for the designer. It is not collegiate behaviour to remain indifferent to the excitement costume designers display when showing you some sample of material. If the actor's skin tones read correctly then what they are wearing should also read correctly. But there is a big proviso in this broad generalisation that should cause the lighting designer to give greater consideration to the 'frocks'.

We 'see' a colour because the range of wavelengths in the light with which we illuminate the object contains those colours. Light containing this colour or wavelength is reflected from the object to our eyes. If there is no red in the spectrum of the source you will not be able to read any red in the material.

This applies not just to the extremes of spectral availability but to minor balances in the colour of the light illuminating the material. I once observed during production rehearsals of *The King and I* that when I added a pale pink wash of light to the existing lighting state for a scene with Anna and the children I was able to make the children's costumes 'pop' without the scene lighting showing it had been altered in any way. What we see is created in our brains and is highly adaptable. Our brains will adjust the perceived image to what we expect to see. A scene suffused with a pink light can feel perfectly clean and white while there is no contrast for the brain to perceive; add some contrasting colour and suddenly the pink reveals itself. However, until that time all the audience's cone receptors get is a stronger signal towards the red end of the spectrum from the additional illumination in that part of the spectrum. Other colours still read but the pinks have 'popped'.

How we read colour also depends on the nature of the reflective surface. A material with a matt finish will produce diffuse reflection—an even reflection of the light from the surface. Shiny surfaces are by definition shiny because of their specular reflection. They work more like a mirror and the colour perceived is not the colour of the material but the colour of the light. Very little that we see on stage is a purely specular surface so there is always a bit of both types of reflection; but costume designers will sometimes choose highly reflective materials for effect; and this is where the lighting designer must be careful to preserve the overall intention of the design. Deep blue light, intended to suggest a rich, exotic night time, might end up turning the leading lady's very expensive dress into something from the under-twelves Irish dancing competition.

For a costume designer good lighting will be that lighting which reproduces the designer's colour palette most accurately. It will treat respectfully the designer's use of shiny fabrics and not rob them of their intrinsic tones. It may follow the lead of the costume designer in the choice of colour palette. It may even enhance the ideas behind the fabric and colour choices the designer has made.

3. Industrial Issues

Welcome to the world of the precariat. Lighting designers, like most theatre practitioners in this country, work on a freelance basis. There is very little job security in any area of professional theatre apart from administration and general arts management. Good steady jobs might be available in client services or marketing or media but if you want to be a theatre 'maker,' be prepared for long periods of unemployment. Theatre performance depends on a large base of unemployed or under-employed talent for its survival. If you want to know who provides the highest proportion of arts subsidy in this country, then I can tell you that it comes from the personal income sacrifice of arts makers. A freelance lighting designer needs to be contracted for around ten productions per annum in order to make something like the average Australian full-time wage. These are the hard facts of life.

Lighting designers always work as part of a creative team. There is a director, a set designer, a costume designer and a lighting designer. Increasingly these days a sound designer will be part of the team and often a composer commissioned to write original music. For musical theatre or opera you would add a choreographer and sometimes a fight director. These people will, in most cases, be individually contracted by a producer or producing company such as one of the state theatre companies. Ultimately we all depend on some full-time administrator enjoying the perks of office space and communications services paid for by others, holiday pay, sick pay, superannuation, expense account, parking, car allowance, somewhere to hang their coat, and tea and biscuits from the company expense account. We are dependent on these administrators to distribute the largesse that enables our survival as freelancers. The opportunity for creative teams to generate their own work opportunities is pretty much limited to the small-scale profit share end of the avant-garde.

So you sit patiently waiting to be chosen as part of the team. Sometimes the initial approach is from the director; more often it is the casting director or artistic administrator of the production company. After an expression of interest and a discussion of dates the financial negotiations begin. For the experienced there will be a pretty standard range of fees and conditions. For others there are guidelines available from the UK-based professional organisation, the Association of Lighting Designers [ALD] or the American United Scenic Artists Union, or from the Australian Production Designers Guild. All publish lists of minimum fees—in the case of the USA these are legally binding union minimums; the ALD's is a guide based on member experience of what companies might expect to pay, the APDG's list is more aspirational. When I got my Tony nomination for *The King and I* I asked my very experienced New York assistant what impact a Tony had on fee levels. 'That plus 25 cents will get you a subway token,' was his cynical and, as I found out, accurate answer.

The payment will usually be a flat fee split into three segments—one on contract signature, another on design submission or rehearsal commencement, and a final payment on opening night. Contracts for commercial productions include a small royalty for the use of the intellectual property (ie your lighting design). Producers prefer this to be a flat weekly figure but designers prefer to negotiate a royalty. For a lighting designer this might be between 0.5% and 1% of proceeds, but a percentage of what is the big question. Once the royalty was a percentage of the gross box office, and for some creative partners it still is; but over the years producers have whittled this down, hedging it around with all sorts of accounting devices. Commercially successful royalty opportunities are the lighting designer's equivalent of winning the lottery and, as in life, these windfalls are extremely rare. Opera companies do not pay royalties apart from those from video sales, but they do pay for lighting designers to return from time to time for revival performances. Revival fees are usually around 60% of the original design fee. Other sources of income for lighting designers are really just cost-covering exercises. Travel expenses, accommodation standards and *per diems* can be areas for negotiation but usually producers fall back on union award rates or on comparative deals struck with other members of the creative team. Producers in the 'for profit' area are always looking to trim costs at the expense of the creative team. Many freelance designers work though an agency, and for many years I did as well, but I came to realise that I no longer had any personal contact with the producing company before turning up on day one. I also soon saw that work invitations mostly came not from agents putting my name forward but from directors who wanted to work with me.

Lighting designers get used to multi-tasking. If we need ten productions in a year then we must keep a number of projects at different levels of development. The first design presentation is usually many months before the rehearsal process starts and would be only a day's participation. At the start of the rehearsal process I will be in the rehearsal studio for three or four days. This enables me to liaise with production staff and be part of the launch of the project. At this time the director and designer will introduce the production ideas to the cast and it is valuable to see and hear the views they put to the rest of the company. Homework or other projects will occupy me for the next few weeks of the rehearsal process but I will spend all of the last week in the rehearsal studio to see the director finally assemble the detailed work of the previous weeks. By this time designing and drafting is done and on-site participation begins. The stage production and preview period is the most intense part of the process and occupies around two weeks. The whole process customarily takes the equivalent of four weeks of full-time work, including a technical production week that almost always runs to 72 hours.

Opening night is the last time I am employed on the project and represents the end of my involvement. A tour or transfer will be separately contracted or covered by an additional clause and payment. Occasionally directors have requested adjustments after opening night and in a collegiate spirit I have usually obliged; but they are not part of the contract and this becomes unpaid work. Is it only in the theatre that people expect a professional of forty years standing to work for nothing?

Designers get used to being on call at any time. Discussions with directors and designers or more commonly email messages are exchanged at all hours of the day, seven days a week. I write this paragraph in a city apartment rented on my behalf by a production company while working on their project. Outside my window office blocks are full of people working at their desks knowing that at five o'clock they will no longer be available to answer questions or re-arrange a schedule or incorporate some new idea into their work. Today is a day that my work calendar shows no activities; but over the coming weekend I am due to spend 18 hours in a darkened theatre. And today, despite no activities scheduled, I am spending several hours discussing with an assistant the planning for next month's production; I have written a number of emails addressing issues about the lighting session this weekend; I have arranged transport and accommodation for my next production; continued via email a negotiation over fee levels for a production in six months' time, adjusted a lighting drawing for yet another production; and amended the documentation for one that I did earlier this year. This is all work that never appears on my schedule and is never counted in the hours of work I do—and yet is essential to my work as a lighting designer.

4. The Technology

The flexibility of modern theatre light sources has seen an exponential growth in the need for light control. When I commenced my lighting career, 60 channels of lighting control was a perfectly adequate installation for most theatres. A channel is like a circuit or a dimmer switch. Sometimes you might need more but 120 channels was considered massive. Contemporary lighting control systems currently employ various versions of a protocol called DMX 512. It allows for the control of 512 channels of information to be sent digitally to dimmers or on board control elements in a moving light. A unit of 512 channels is called a single universe of dmx. Lighting desks like the German built MA2 can control 256 universes—that is the equivalent of 65,536 parameters or channels of information. A parameter could be intensity, which was once the only thing we could control, but it can also be the whole multitude of information that a modern moving light requires. This can be a lot of information. For example the Vari-Lite VL4000 spot (around $25,000 each at your local store) is normally configured to require 57 channels of information. That means just one single light can require nearly as much information as a whole theatre full of lights from the 1970s.

This massive growth in the amount of information that

must be stored and processed for theatre lighting design has triggered several developments. Lighting design as a separate creative discipline sprang from a response to the rapid expansion in lighting technology in the 1950s as part of the technology boom. Suddenly there were simply too many lights to deal with by shouting at the theatre electrician. Contemporary lighting design faces a similar problem and this has led to the development of specialist lighting programmers. Programmers deal with the data manipulation of all the multiple parameters required by a lighting rig with moving lights. There is simply too much data for the lighting designer to deal with while maintaining focus on the overall stage picture. Any lighting designer working on a large scale project will be very careful to ensure that they have a very fast, accurate, user-friendly programmer on board.

Huge data loads in turn led to the development of new types of lighting control. Lighting desks built to control 60 channels in the 1970s would have an individual fader for each channel and these faders would be duplicated or triplicated with separate master faders. The master fader would give overall control of the subset of individual faders. Each stage image would be created from the intensity of 60 faders, laboriously written down with pencil and paper by the operator, who then moved on to the next and so on. Multiple 'presets' allowed separate scenes to be set up beforehand and then faded in on the masters: the operator would prepare their own hand-written operating plot to replay the lighting cues during the course of the performance. Changes by the designer in the course of developing the design could then cause havoc in the careful documents the operator had prepared.

The recording of cues was what might be termed a 'snapshot' approach to the lighting design. Each image was recorded in full detail and played back. The trouble with this method was that it made it hard to maintain continuity in a performance. Imagine, for example, a production with a hundred lighting images or cues, In each one there is a single area constantly lit. To amend the intensity of light in its area a hundred individual cues must be updated. There is just too much extraneous information. It becomes a huge problem with moving lights when a snapshot image records values for all sorts of parameters that do not need to change from cue to cue—parameters that, unlike a dimmer intensity, are not actually seen. The compression algorithms of modern software, whether jpeg or mp3, are about removing this redundant information. This is what modern desks try to do: in current philosophy it is termed 'tracking'. Only the parameters that actually change from cue to cue are recorded, in other words each parameter of each light stays where it is until it gets an instruction to do something else.

These days all my drafting is done by computer, in fact everything I do is by computer. I no longer print a plan but email it to the production management. I don't even have a printed plan on the production desk but work straight from my computer screen. I adjust the drawing as I go, amending the cue synopsis and keeping all my documentation up to date. I even prefer to do my cue placement notes directly into the script in pdf form on my computer. I am not sure when I switched entirely to CAD but it was around twenty years ago.

And yet there is much more to come with lighting design and computer systems. I have used quite a few times a 3D visualisation software called ESP Vision in which it is possible to create lighting cues in a 3D computer model of the set. The Royal Opera House has a very good system. I once used it to light an entire musical while sitting in a hotel room in Perth; and when the show had its first preview in Korea two months later the second half of the show was exactly as I had left it. There was no time for improvement and although the result would not have won any awards at least we could see the actors, and the cues went in the right place and we got on with the show. This is where the future will be: the capacity to light a show on your laptop while sitting in rehearsal. Imagine being able to show that to the director and the actors! The lighting designer's equivalent of the set designer's model box.

5. The Opinions

So with all this preparation, the creativity, the ingenuity, the technology and the hard labour, what are we left with at the end of the run? The reviews. It is well known that a bad review on Broadway from the *New York Times'* Ben Brantley can kill a commercial musical stone dead. So should we perhaps consider the critic as the ultimate arbiter of what is good lighting? After all, the critic should be the person best informed about the text, the production, the quality of the acting, direction and design. They should have seen more theatre than any of us, they should understand the nature of the process and be able to present the informed views of the general theatre-going public. Furthermore the critic can rank the success of this performance against the many others they may have seen and heard.

But the effectiveness of the lighting may be the one area the critic is not too sure about. Perhaps because it is an area about which it is hard to have an opinion. An opinion about a design or a performance implies having some understanding of how it might have been, or of how it falls short of your imagined performance. It is hard to do this with lighting. Most people take their lit environment for granted. If it does not draw attention to itself the lighting will always manage to sneak under the critical radar. A critic may not fully understand the vocal techniques of the soprano but can express a view as to whether the composer's score had been satisfactorily reproduced. In the lighting design there is no pre-existing score and hence little for the critic to test against. Except that there is, it is called the text and it is the dialogue the performers use to convey their world.

Lighting does not come in for a lot of criticism and lighting designers are thankful for that. The accepted view in the industry is that if the lighting has not made itself noticeable then it must have blended well with the production and served the needs of the performance. Yet sometimes we do get a review. If it is one like my mother might have written then we are well pleased. Sometimes, however, a review might be so downright confusing about what the writer has seen that you might take it for a different production. I recently had a review in Adelaide for a production of *Vere (Faith)*, by John Doyle, a sadly comic study of a physicist diagnosed with early-onset dementia, in which he described my lighting thus: 'Nigel Levings' lighting is uncharacteristically mucky and not well explained.'[28] I was pleased that it was uncharacteristic of me but the review was headed by a crystal clear photo of the cast in action, each face sharply modeled, each actor's thoughts clearly visible on their faces, the room itself sharply characterised by a powerful shaft of light through clerestory windows. I had assumed the intended word had been 'murky' not 'mucky' as my dictionary gives mucky to mean 'covered with dirt or filth'; or perhaps, in the British colloquial sense, 'mildly pornographic'!

I concede the 'not well explained' point and in this I am

not suggesting—nor, I assume, was the reviewer—that there should have been subtitles or footnotes to the lighting plot. In the production I had attempted to suggest something of the progress of the central character's dementia. To find a way to suggest Vere's extreme confusion as the condition went about its task of destroying his agile mind. If the overall production fails to convey this to the critic then the lighting will indeed be 'not well explained'.

So what is good lighting from a critic's point of view? We can be pretty sure that the seat allocated will be one of the better seats in the house. It will be close enough so that visibility should not be an issue, central, and close enough to the same lighting angles as were set from the production desk. An experienced critic will have expectations of the designer's work; and their understanding of the textual requirements of the lighting should be greater than that of the average audience member. In this case they should appreciate the instances where it is clear that the lighting designer has given thought to the demands of the text. I would suggest that it is the integration of the lighting design within the production's overall telling of the text that ultimately should mark the lighting as 'good' in the eyes of the critic.

6. The Lighting Designer and Good Lighting

On home turf at last and I am pretty clear about what I consider to be good lighting. Visibility is the first marker and I am rarely satisfied with this aspect of my work. In the process of the lighting sessions I am searching for shape and atmosphere and coverage and linkages; it is opening night before I get the opportunity to sit back and watch. Each opening night for me is attended with great anxiety about the levels of visibility from moment to moment. I feel the internal tension rising as I watch an actor move into an area that seems not quite clear and crisp to me. And yet just what level of visibility is acceptable is tricky. Since it is a sliding scale perhaps there is no exact point, just as there is no agreed viewpoint and no perfect visual system. It is a highly subjective judgment.

I have tried to apply a few tests over the years. Can you tell, by this light, whether the actor is laughing or crying? If you could tell would you care? What about the non-speaking actor's response to the speaker? Can you tell from their expression and body language what they are feeling? Do they believe to be accurate what the other actor is telling them? These are little visibility tests that we can apply. They tell us how well the actors are able to communicate from moment to moment.

When setting the placement of lighting cues I am looking to mark the 'hinge' moments in the text, those points where the characters' lives change forever. This is about structuring the cue sequence, getting the flow of light to make sense in terms of how the scene is playing. Getting the placement of the cues precisely right and matching the timing to the right tempo for that specific moment. In these days of increasingly sophisticated control over the timing of a lighting transition it may even involve minute time differences in the dissolve of individual lights—and this in a lighting rig that could easily encompass several hundred individual lights.

Current lighting control systems allow extremely complicated manipulation of the transition from one lighting image to the next. We are now well in reach of that dream of a totally fluid light plot, one in which the light never ceases to shift over the entire course of the play. This unceasing play of light already happens in the hectic world of rock and roll lighting, of course, but I am talking about a subtle flow of light, perhaps even imperceptible beyond the realisation that at each moment the focus is on the actor driving the scene. One marker of good lighting for me is how well this flow of light works through the play. If it seems lumpy and awkward this is disturbing but if it fits the pace and meaning of the text then it should appear seamless. Better still if you 'didn't notice that the lights had changed.'

A personal marker for me is the recognition that the lighting rig I created has worked to its maximum capacity. If lighting is analogous to painting then the lighting rig is the designer's equivalent of the artist's palette. The drawback to this particular palette is that before we make the painting we have to decide on what colours and how much of each. The conditions of this game require that once inside our 'studio' we cannot add to what we have brought in on the palette. Our studio, unlike the artist's, does not contain boxes filled with the paints and brushes we have accumulated. We have only our plan and the lighting rig—that is the placement of particular types of lighting instruments in specific places around the theatre. The only wiggle room we have is the chance to alter how we intended to use a particular 'colour'/lighting instrument. The recycling of spare instruments can often lift a design from 'struggling' to 'good'. The rig is good when it is fit for the purpose. And the purpose is to illuminate the performance.

Good lighting is intelligent lighting. That is what I really like to see. Lighting that indicates deep thought about the text and the director's interpretation of that text. The lighting can display intelligent thought in a number of ways. It can be seen in the precision with which the lighting shifts relate to the ideas expressed in the text. It can be seen in the style of lighting chosen: it might be a highly expressionist form, heightened naturalism, pure abstracted illumination, historically referenced, contemporary industrial, architecturally accurate, perhaps the expression of a detailed world outside the stage space that intrudes and illuminates the performance space. It can be seen when we detect some density of meaning; something poetic in the way the lighting changes have rhythm; in the way the light sets up images and then opens them out to reveal a deeper understanding; in the way the light is shaped to the narrative and its resolution. Intelligent light sculpts a three-dimensional architecture within the stage—or rather a four-dimensional space since the flow of time is a critical aspect of the design.

What skills do we need?

What skills are required of the theatre lighting designer at the beginning of the twenty-first century? Can you teach them? Or are we born to light? A creative life spent at the interface of art and technology breeds a very particular kind of artist and requires a very special set of skills. This is an attempt to describe the perfectly 'fit' lighting designer by listing the skills and knowledge they should possess.

- Firstly you should be able to work calmly and quickly under extreme time pressure, to have the capacity to concentrate even when surrounded by distractions and to do this while maintaining a courteous and professional demeanour. Your work ethic should allow for the adherence to demanding deadlines for the supply of technical information regarding a design.

- You need to be capable of making both spontaneous and planned creative decisions. Your vision should be sharp enough to take in at an instant all the details of a large and

flowing composition of bodies, scenery and light
and be able to quickly and intuitively respond.
You must have the creative skill and dexterity
to improvise on an underlying design theme.

- You should have a deep understanding
  of literature and an ability to quickly
  comprehend both the surface meaning of a
  text and its underlying subtext. A solid grasp
  of the historical context of theatrical texts and
  associated performance styles (the dramaturgy).
  You should be able to read or at least follow a
  music score. It is critical that you are able to
  respond to the emotional flow of a musical
  work: you have to feel it in your heart.

- You will need collaborative work methods
  combined with the ability to take a strong
  leadership role. To have empathy for the
  demands faced by performers and be willing
  to adapt. You should be able to communicate
  abstract ideas in a coherent manner. Deliver
  clear instructions to technical staff in a way that
  opens channels for their creative contribution.
  You will need a broad understanding of the
  latest theatre technology and an ability to
  speak the language of that technology.

- In practical terms you should have knowledge
  of the physics of light, how it is produced
  and how it behaves. Understand the biology

of vision, of how the eye works and a psychological understanding of the process of perception. A broad understanding of electricity and electronics. Familiarity with computer programming skills in CAD, spreadsheets, specialist control system programming, word processing, visualisation software and image manipulation software.

- Above all—you need a thick skin and a not-easily-bruised ego.

Some of the attributes in this list can be learned at educational institutions but it is my belief that the most critical aspects are innate and revealed or developed where we work—at the interface of art and technology.

Theatre is above all a collaborative art form. This is what sometimes allows it to become such a transcendent experience for an audience. If you can get all your collaborations right then the overall artistic result will be so much more than could be achieved by a single *auteur*.[29] But the chemistry of human interactions in the pressure cooker of creativity is hard to predict. Creative teams in the entertainment industry tend to hunt in packs. Once you find the team you like to work with, you stick together. Mutual unspoken understandings develop, shorthand discussions, and above all trust, builds within the team and the common artistic goal becomes clear and achievable. Opera as a theatre form is particularly dependent on the artistic collaboration of the team and their complexity makes it harder to assemble the right combination of personalities, particularly as the critical musical elements of the production will usually be contracted long before the production team. Opera also suffers from tighter production schedules than other theatre forms. It is an expensive art form, in expensive buildings, and really only transcends when cast at the most expensive end of the pool of performers. However, if you get all those collaborations right, then the experience for the audience may well be one that holds them for life.

In short, here is how I think we can judge quality in theatre lighting design:

- By what degree the visibility accords
  with the intentions of the production;

- How closely the lighting integrates with
  the design vision of that production;

- How clearly it helps reveal the
  deeper meaning of the text;

- The visual pleasure it offers to its audience.

Quality in light as a tool for use is a decision for the designer about what tools are at their disposal. It is to a large extent budget-dependent and lighting designers would do well to learn to work with less flexible and cheaper instruments. The fundamental design decisions start with the relationship between the rigged position of the light, the acting space and the audience point of view. In that sense, where the light comes from is more important than what it comes from. The light source itself is neither good nor bad: the way in which it is used and the appropriateness of this use is the sole basis for any judgment about the quality of the light source.

Quality in light control is dependent on the ease and speed with which the designer can deal quickly with the broad brush issues of creating the design while providing the greatest degree of extremely fine control over the flow of light through the course of a performance. In this case the development of lighting control systems and philosophies is very definitely evolutionary. Survival of the fittest leads lighting designers to look to the latest developments; one big proviso sounds a warning—never buy Version One of anything.

Quality for the lighting designer is ultimately to do with their collaborators, with personal relationships under pressure-cooker conditions. Nobody casts the lighting designer first or even second or third in the creative partnership so it is virtually impossible to generate your own work. A proven ability to get the job done on time counts for a lot. Creative acts of genius may or may not come but if the show opens on time, on budget and without too many displays of temperament, then the producers will be happy and you may get another invitation to collaborate.

Time pressures in the theatre production period usually mean there is very little opportunity for the leisurely exploration of everyone's ideas about the lighting. Sometimes it is possible to create a series of sketch lighting states to indicate to the rest of the team in what direction the design might progress; but more often it is simply a race to get the data into the desk. The essence of the creative collaboration is trust. Trust that the first images produced are just that, first thoughts and not the finished design. Trust that the lighting designer's process is similar to the set designer's, in that each lighting cue will have many drafts before a final set of images is ready for an audience. As with the set design process, a concept sketch will sometimes get developed a very long way before the realisation dawns that a different approach might be better. For the lighting designer this realisation will often come way too late for any practical resolution. A new approach might require a different lighting rig and no producer will willingly pay for that process. To push the existing lighting rig as far as it can go in the service of the production is the best you can do. Good teams trust that a process of mutual support gets the best results. Micro-management by others only results in suffocating the creative inspiration. Judgment about who is a good lighting designer is probably an assessment best made by the rest of the creative team.

Looking back on a career spanning forty-five years of professional lighting design and over 490 productions, my overwhelming thought is a lament that I have not yet done my best work. A sense of resentment that circumstances and our country's lack of respect for late career artists has deprived me of a chance to put all that I have learned and all the skills I have honed into my contribution to some new great work for the theatre. I long to once more work with the best of the best on some truly significant work for the theatre. I am grateful, however, that time and circumstances allowed me to work with such a wonderful and disparate collection of directors on some truly memorable works. To Moshinsky and Armfield and Kosky and Sharman and Luhrmann and Wherrett and Ogilvie and Copley and Judge and Cox and Caird and Jarvefelt, and with apologies to any of the other 119 directors with whom I have worked, I say thanks.

The play of light on surface continues to be a source of constant delight and almost physical pleasure for me, an inspiration for my work. When I get it right, even if only to my partial satisfaction, my lighting design springs from a desire to share with an audience this love of light: visibility, poetic density of meaning—but above all pure, succulent, sensuous visual pleasure.

Endnotes

1   *Camelot,* musical, book and lyrics by Alan Jay Lerner, music by Frederick Loewe.

2   A scene cut in later productions of this work.

3   *The Government Inspector,* satirical play by Nikolai Gogol.

4   *Chicago,* , musical, book by Bob Fosse, music by John Kander, lyrics by Fred Ebb.

5   Brendan Behan, Irish Republican, poet, short story writer, novelist, and playwright, best remembered for his play *The Hostage* and his drinking. .

6   Now the State Theatre Company of South Australia.

7   Robert Helpmann's ballet *Sun Music* from the score by Peter Sculthorpe, premiered in Sydney on 2 August 1968 at Her Majesty's Theatre. The designer was Kenneth Rowell.

8   *La Sonnambula,* opera in the bel canto tradition by Bellini.

9   *Volpone,* comedy by Ben Jonson; co-directed by John Bell, who also played the title role.

10 Known as Opera Australia from 1996.

11 *The Magic Flute,* opera by Mozart.

12 *Falstaff,* opera by Verdi.

13 *Fidelio,* opera with spoken dialogue by Beethoven.

14 *A Christmas Carol,* staged adaptation of the short story by Charles Dickens. Directed by Ian Judge. Included in the cast was Australian actor Philip Quast.

15 *West Side Story,* musical book by Arthur Laurents, music by Leonard Bernstein, lyrics by Stephen Sondheim.

16 *Don Giovanni* and *Cosi Fan Tutte,* operas by Mozart.

17 *Regietheater,* or 'director's theatre', a contemporary theatre practice that chooses to ignore authorial intention regarding textual given circumstances.

18 Frenchman Patrice Chéreau's landmark centenary production of Wagner's *Der Ring des Nibelungen* in 1976 at Bayreuth.

19 *L'Orfeo* [*La favola d'Orfeo*], opera by Monteverdi.

20 *Die tote Stadt* (*The Dead City*), opera by Erich Wolfgang Korngold.

21 'Pepper's ghost' is a theatrical illusion technique named after John Henry Pepper, a scientist who popularized the effect in a famed demonstration in 1862.

22 *La Bohème,* opera by Puccini. Stage and screen director Baz Luhrmann updated the setting from the 1840s to 1957 Paris for his production by Opera Australia in 2002. It transferred to Broadway and Levings' design won the Outer Critics Circle Award, Drama Desk Award, and Tony Award for Best Lighting Design in 2003, and Ovation Award in 2004.

23 *The King and I,* musical, music by Richard Rodgers, book and lyrics by Oscar Hammerstein. Levings' design for *The King and I* won the Outer Critics Circle Award and was nominated for both the Drama Desk Award and the Tony Award for Best Lighting Design.

24 Stephen Curtis, *The Designer: Decorator or Dramaturg?* Platform Papers 46, February 2016.

25 https://commons.wikimedia.org/wiki/File:Ilya_Repin_Unexpected_visitors.jpg

26 https://commons.wikimedia.org/wiki/File:Mona_Lisa.jpg

27 *Company,* musical, book by George Furth, music and lyrics by Stephen Sondheim.

28 Tim Lloyd, review, 'John Doyle's *Vere (Faith)* for State Theatre Company tackles big themes with wry comedy', *Advertiser,* 17 October 2013.

29 *Auteur,* a theatre- or filmmaker whose stylistic influence and practice is so distinctive they rank as the work's author.

FORCHCOMING

PP No. 50, February 2017
A RESTLESS GIANT: Challenges
from Regional Australia
Lindy Hume

Leading opera, theatre and festival director Lindy Hume begins her assessment of the arts in regional Australia with a return to Lyndon Terracini's 2007 Platform Paper, *A Regional State of Mind, Making Art Outside Metropolitan Australia* and finds it prescient. But now amid the shifting plates of the arts in 2017, she challenges some of his concepts. Through colourful portraits of artistic innovation in small towns and communities, Hume traces the rise of a more assertive, even radical regional state of mind. Hume likens these enterprises, found in locations thousands of kilometers apart, to the stirrings of a restless giant: a rebellious counter-urban movement ready to make a profound impact on the national culture. As an artist living in regional Australia, she finds it an ideal place to develop new performance work, and argues that more flow and greater integration between the regional and metropolitan arts ecosystems could, over time, reshape Australia's cultural identity.

AT YOUR LOCAL BOOKSHOP FROM 1 FEBRUARY
AND AS A PAPERBACK OR ONLINE FROM
OUR WEBSITE AT
WWW.CURRENCYHOUSE.ORG.AU

Copyright Information

PLATFORM PAPERS
Quarterly essays from Currency House Inc.
Founding Editor: Dr John Golder
Editor: Katharine Brisbane
Currency House Inc. is a non-profit association and resource centre advocating the role of the performing arts in public life by research, debate and publication.

Postal address: PO Box 2270, Strawberry Hills, NSW 2012, Australia
Email: info@currencyhouse.org.au Tel: (02) 9319 4953
Website: www.currencyhouse.org.au Fax: (02) 9319 3649

Editorial Committee: Katharine Brisbane AM, Michael Campbell, Dr Robin Derricourt, Professor Julian Meyrick, Martin Portus, Dr Nick Shimmin, Greig Tillotson

THE LIGHTING DESIGNER: WHAT IS 'GOOD LIGHTING'?

ISBN 978 0 9946130 1 1
ISSN 1449-583X

Typeset in Garamond
Printed by McPherson's Printing Group
Production by XOU Creative